COMPANION
PLANTING

COMPANION PLANTING

·Bob Flowerdew·

Kyle Cathie Limited

This paperback edition published in Great
Britain in 2018 by Kyle Cathie Limited
Part of Octopus Publishing Group Limited
Carmelite House, 50 Victoria Embankment
London EC4Y 0SZ
www.kylebooks.co.uk

First published in hardback in 2010

Text 2010 © Bob Flowerdew
Design 2010 © Kyle Cathie Limited
Photography 2010 © Peter Cassidy
Illustration 2010 © Alison Clements

ISBN 978-0-85783-468-3

10 9 8 7 6 5 4 3 2 1

A Cataloguing in Publication record for this title
is available from the British Library.

Photography: Peter Cassidy
Illustrations: Alison Clements
Design: Louise Leffler
Project Editor: Sophie Allen
Copy Editor: Helena Caldon

Photographic Acknowledgements:
All photography by Peter Cassidy except
pp. 7, 11, 67, 73, 91 by Bob Flowerdew

Printed in China by 1010 Printing Ltd

Contents

Introduction

The more I've investigated the more I'm convinced that understanding plant interactions with each other and all associated creatures, big and small, is crucial. All have evolved together over countless millions of years. Each have adjusted to the others' presence; with each adapting entirely for its own benefit and, however inadvertently, sometimes helping another.

Plants behave much like us; some get on with others, some don't, many are indifferent, and all may change depending on the time and place. Indeed, it would be very strange if every plant were to grow totally independently as if each were in its own test tube. Of the many tens of thousands of plants found and cultivated in our gardens, would it not be really bizarre if not one of them had some effect on another or aided another's friend or foe?

Observed by gardeners over millennia there's a huge body of anecdotal evidence for plant companionships. Yet, these interactions are ignored by a blinkered science that insists on trialling everything in isolation away from the very environment it already does, or soon will, live in. Allegedly, 'scientific' writers have dismissed companion planting as little more than superstitious mumbo jumbo and studiously ignore the ancient and still common agricultural practice of mixing cereal and leguminous crops to gain a fifth more total yields. They manage to overlook the effectiveness of mixed planting in the Tropics where

Right: Aromatic herbs beneath benefit apples in multiple ways, and look good

growing monocrops often disastrously fails from rampant pests and diseases. And, obviously, they've never noticed that farmers encourage mixed herbage; add clover to boost their grasses and sow alfalfa in their orchards to access deeply buried minerals.

Now, I admit, there is still much to be understood, but the general principles are established. Plants interact with each other, and with creatures around them, in many ways, and once we know what is happening we may use it to our advantage. A good example is the leguminous pea and bean family, whose members usually create a fertility surplus. By interplanting legumes with other more demanding plants we satisfy the latter's needs without continuing effort or expense. So sweet peas, lupins, brooms, laburnums and many others help feed other flowers around them, and peas and French beans feed your cabbages and sweet corn. Simultaneously, this mingling misleads and confuses pests and obstructs the spread of diseases. However, we also need to be aware that not all plants get on. For example, some of the allium family are unhappy growing near some legumes; i.e. onions do not do well near beans, and vice versa.

So, this book is about all these many and varied companion effects and how we can utilise them for our ends, and includes a judicious selection of which plants to grow together. After all, we all want more beautiful tasty crops and flowers with less input. So let's allow the plants and wildlife to do much of the work for us – not just by working with nature but by harnessing it, all in the gentlest possible way.

Left: Lupins can be great companions - they supply other plants with nitrates - and suppress weeds and other seeds from germinating nearby

So what is companion planting?

Simply, it is no more than carefully choosing which plants to grow with, before or after each other, or planting and sowing nearby those that are known to get on with each other or offer some benefit to another, such as enhancing fertility or handicapping pests or diseases. It also means avoiding putting known 'enemies' together.

It is a faint effect – rarely does it offer 'instant cures' – however, most of gardening is about improving things at the margin and likewise with companion planting. Gardening is often about adjusting the conditions to suit the plant, and companion planting is just one more method of adjustment. Different companions can aid or hinder those around them in a multitude of minute ways. However, many small improvements eventually stack up to give better crops and flowers on healthier, more robust plants.

The great scientist Charles Darwin gave an excellent example of such a faint effect with his tale of old ladies, cats and clover. He explained that meadows around a village with proportionately more old ladies would give bigger crops of hay. His reasoning was that old ladies keep cats, therefore more old ladies means more cats. Cats catch mice, therefore more cats soon leads to less mice. Mice raid bumble and humble bee nests, therefore less mice equals more bees. These bees are needed to fertilise clover, therefore more bees generates more clover. Clover

Right: Nestling amongst brassicas benefits this pepper, keeping its roots cool and shady, sheltering it from winds, yet its head is well exposed to sun and air

is leguminous and feeds grasses, which grow more luxuriantly in its company. So, more old ladies mean more cats, less mice, more bees, more clover, more grass and, thus, bigger crops of hay.

In a similar fashion we can simply grow certain wild or garden flowers and these then sustain beneficial insects between the crops who need them for pollination. Other companions may aid predators or parasites with shelter, nectar or pollen or even suffer pests just to feed our friends. We can choose companions to help improve fertility generally or specifically, or simply to provide support or shelter. Each companion only contributes a little but, overall, the effect is

Clover, bees and grasses have evolved together with mutual advantages, each does much better with, rather than without, the others

cumulative and our plants can prosper where otherwise they may only have survived.

Nonetheless, positive companion effects are usually relatively small and are far outweighed by the much greater importance of good gardening methods. Companion planting is not a substitute for good feeding and watering, or weeding and pruning correctly, it will rarely enable an entirely unsuitable choice to thrive, though it may help the less suitable be a little less uncomfortable. I strongly suggest you make every effort to be a good gardener before you rely on companion effects. Even so, it is worth reading on and noting which plants get on but, even more importantly, to be aware of which fail to get on together, as it is crucial to at least avoid those combinations.

Why did companion planting interactions arise?

Plants do not grow in our gardens as they do in nature. We choose their soil, site and positioning in sun, shade, damp or drought; we feed, water and prune and reduce their competition from other plants. Thus, we help plants thrive in places in which they would not ordinarily survive. We also provide the best places for germination; in nature, seeds are distributed prolifically, only those few finding suitable spots succeed in germinating, emerging and growing into mature specimens, conditions we can approximately recreate for them.

Plants that enjoy similar conditions naturally occur together. One of the factors affecting their success in the wild is the interactions with those other plants around about them. So, over aeons natural groupings of plants that fit well together and with their local conditions have evolved to make up the different plantscapes we take for granted. As you travel, you notice different mixtures of plants compose heaths and meadows, woodland and alpine screes; the composition in one place seldom contains many members from different areas. A condition such as, say, acid soil excludes lovers of alkaline soils and vice versa. The place and its conditions naturally selects for those most suitable plants, which must inevitably be similar mixes for similar situations. Each plant then has come to 'expect' certain other plants and creatures to be there in its surroundings, yet we put together plants from many countries and diverse regions in our gardens where they are no longer surrounded by their expected associates.

No wonder, then, that some may not do as well as we think they should. For instance, a common difficulty is establishing wild orchids. It's been discovered many orchids cannot succeed without certain soil fungi – and these may themselves only exist where other plants with their associated micro-life create suitable conditions for them. Likewise, alfalfa aka Lucerne (medicago), is a very deep-rooting and productive fodder legume especially useful for its mineral-mining abilities, but it cannot grow in many soils unless the right fungi are also present. (These can now be provided commercially with the seed.) This need for accompanying fungi, mycorrhizal as they're called, is very much a major cause and tool of many companion interactions.

Above: Many orchids can only grow if they have the right companion fungi

History and mythology

Greek and Roman writers observed that some plants did and did not get on together – and they were particularly careful to note those affecting their grapevines! Cabbages, laurels and radishes were all considered detrimental to their beloved grapes; likewise, oaks were considered bad to grow near olives, walnuts made the ground sterile and lupins suppressed weeds. Pliny the Elder most perceptively observed the competition between plants and wrote of how they deprived each other of nourishment with thicknesses of leaves (probably meaning their shade). He also deduced they put out scents and juices to handicap rivals. He advocated mixing vetches with turnips and chickpeas with cabbages in order to keep away caterpillars – an excellent piece of advice that worked then and now.

Over the following centuries, the learned read his works but they were seldom gardeners. Gardening almost expired during the Dark Ages, with only the monasteries sustaining some planting, mostly medicinal. In medieval times, the crusaders revived some interest in horticulture from their contact with Arabic culture. Their archetypal enclosed flower garden around a central water feature became a dominant influence that is still copied today. With increasing travel to the Middle East, new plants, mostly medicinal, made their way to Europe – some from as far as India and China via the Silk Route. However, although plants arrived, the knowledge of gardening methods rarely did. Indeed, it's even recorded that when tea first arrived it was diligently prepared, the liquid discarded and the soggy leaves ardently and errantly consumed!

Right: Strawberries utilising the same pot as a grapevine - not only a bonus crop, they indicate attacks of weevil, by succumbing first, and of scale infestations from sooty mould appearing on their leaves. The chickweed helps keep the compost covered

The Chinese had been farming intensively for many thousands of years and we could have gained greatly by studying their methods earlier. They continually interplanted different crops to maximise yields and their recycling of all wastes was exemplary. Interestingly, in China they grew barley and Chinese clover (a form of alfalfa/Lucerne) together and mixed cereals with beans. It would be exciting to discover how and when the similar mixed crops of old English farming (known as Maslin or Dredge) of intersown cereals and beans originated.

Increasing commerce with the Far East only added new plants sparingly, then gardening changed abruptly with the stupendous discovery of the New World introducing a host of new plants to European gardeners, multiplying their crops and flowers overnight. As with the Far Eastern crops, some of these had been grown for millennia intermixed as companions. In particular, native Americans interplanted their most important crops, The Three Sisters – corn (maize), beans (French and runner) and cucurbits (squashes) – and traditionally grew them together, not separately. These plants still get on exceptionally well together, even in much cooler, less sunny countries, such as southern England.

Sadly, few European gardeners took much notice of such 'myths' and companion effects remained relatively unnoticed until more recent times. An early pioneer, Jethro Tull, studied the damaging effects of weed competition and counteracted it with his novel seed drill followed by precision horse hoeing. Lord 'Turnip' Townsend introduced the concept of rotation with his four-fold sequence of a grazed clover ley (thus mucked), followed by successive crops of wheat, turnips (or other roots) and barley before another ley started the cycle over again. However, garden practices remained unaffected, or at least they did here in England. On the other side of the Channel, French market gardeners were carefully keeping foes apart and growing compatible crops together – much like Chinese farmers. Cabbages, celery, cauliflowers and lettuces were interplanted in the open, as were endives, onions, spinach, strawberries and turnips. In the even more valuable space under bell jars they mixed together carrots, cauliflowers, lettuces, radishes and turnips with an intensity we can barely imagine. By employing immense quantities of manure a Monsieur Ponce recorded sales of 20,000lbs of carrots, 20,000lbs of onions, 6,000 heads of cabbage, 3,000 heads of cauliflower, 5,000 baskets of tomatoes, 5,000 baskets of

Right: The Three Sisters, sweet corn, beans, and squash, have thrived together since their original cultivation in the ancient New World

Bob's beds - forty of them; each carries a herb or vegetable crop with companions

choice fruit and 154,000 heads of salad in a year – all from well under three acres.

One important reason why the Continentals have observed companion effects more than the British was Jethro Tull's seed drill. In Britain, this led to the widespread agricultural sowing of long, straight parallel rows – soon copied by gardeners. We still do exactly this on most vegetable plots, however, on the Continent, farmers, and thence gardeners, were not so keen to adopt this new row and hoe method. The gardeners in particular continued their practice of growing crops in small rectangular blocks. Now, whereas it is hard to spot faint interactions between parallel rows of different crops, the varying effect across a block with different companions on opposite sides may be very apparent; thus, far more companion effects were noted. So we find companion planting is now employed more by Continental Bio-dynamic gardening than by the very similar British-based system of organic gardening.

The Victorians, in awe of the new science of chemistry, became entangled with a quixotic search for effective pesticides, herbicides, fungicides and so on and they rarely considered the interplay of the plants themselves. Indeed, they deliberately confined all experiment to the test tube 'to remove the vicissitudes of nature' – the very things of most interest! But gardeners still planted cabbages between celery trenches to avoid the caterpillars, used potatoes to lure wireworms from hops, noted how certain weeds harboured problems and how insectivorous birds were controlling aphids and other pests.

Knowledge from other cultures slowly mingled as foreign travel increased. Returning colonial adventurers brought back first-hand experience of the tropical situation where plants had long been used as nurse and shade companions. Where it is hot or bright, many crops need to be grown in the shade, coffee especially so, and suitable shady trees are employed for just this purpose. In our shorter, cooler growing season it may still help lettuce or spinach to be in the shade of peas or beans. And tropical heat also drives pests and diseases at a furious rate, so there are serious difficulties with mono-cultured crops. Thus, traditionally, several crops were interplanted with compatible plants continuously maturing, being removed and replaced by others. The best of such systems produced huge amounts of food for millennia, albeit at a cost of huge amounts of hands-on human labour.

Today, strident voices deceive us of the world's choices. We're fobbed off with platitudes of 'feeding the poor' and 'saving the planet' if we only adopt genetically modified seeds, dearly bought technology and yet more toxic chemicals. A better answer lies in simpler, established solutions of known companion crops; soil fertilised with green manures and compost, surrounded by hedges of other companions, and all giving more crops, shelter and pest control for free. But then there's no product to sell, so such rewarding lines of investigation are seldom pursued. In practice it's sadly in the interests of 'agri-chemi-medi-govern-corporations' to dissuade folk even of the health benefits of wholesome organic food, and so, predictably, very little research has been or is being done in any such area. How much less could such combined vested interest want it confirmed that simply growing the right plants together would enable us to dispense with almost all of their fertilisers, pesticides, additives and drugs?

Ecology, bootstraps and succession

As was explained before, the conditions of any given place naturally select for certain well-suited collections of plants. The study of these and their associated wildlife is called ecology. Unfortunately, there was originally much confusion over the role of what are now known as mycorrhizal root fungi. These were misguidedly considered pathological infections and not valuable partners. It was only with more sensitive investigation that their true role has been uncovered. The majority of plants have these symbiotic associations and usually not with just one but with several different fungi and bacteria – some pine trees have hundreds. Again, these vary with soil conditions. However, their role is consistent: the fungi gain carbohydrates from the plants and, in return, provide the plants with soil nutrients more efficiently than the plant roots can obtain them on their own. Ironically, the group of plants that have been most intensively investigated by agri-science are the cereals, the very group with the fewest such associations.

And nature does not stand still but it lifts itself by its own bootstraps. The plants growing together on one spot slowly change the conditions there until eventually they are no longer as well suited to it. As their appropriateness decreases, other more fitting plants succeed

Right: A well kempt garden would soon become a forest if left to itself

them. Now, in nature, this is usually in the direction of richer soils with more complexity of life above and below ground. Bare rock is weathered and, at first, lichens and mosses may be the only life to gain a foothold and these slowly create a soil from their own decaying remains and by-products – though with excessive water, a peat bog may result at first. However, as time continues, first small 'weeds' then bigger perennials and woodier, longer-lived plants become prevalent, each changing the conditions until another form supersedes the existing occupants. Eventually, over time, the continuous enrichment usually results in a forest. You can observe the same process in any derelict garden. Soon grasses and stinging nettles choke out everything else, then brambles and small shrubs creep in until, within a very short time, trees start to take over.

This inexorable process is called succession and we gardeners are continually fighting against it. We do not want our bare vegetable or herbaceous bed to grow to trees but to be full of our chosen plants. Yet, nature abhors bare soil, so 'weed' seeds in the soil first try to recover the ground while others blown in may aid them. We must continuously prevent them getting away, and an easy way to do this is to go along with succession and to fill the beds with well-mulched herbaceous plants that fill the ground entirely, leaving little space for 'weeds'.

However, herbaceous plants die down in winter and are still prone to being overcome by more enduring plants. The next stage in succession is shrubby woody plants and a bed of these is even easier to 'keep clean'. The conditions they create, particularly the shade and leaf litter underneath, disadvantage most other plants. The shrubs would be supplanted by climbers, and eventually by trees, but shrubs, especially evergreens, give temporary relief which lasts many years and is sufficient for most gardeners. To recap: a neglected shrub bed, especially if mulched, will stay cleaner and tidier longer than an untended vegetable bed. But you probably knew that anyway...

The whole point is this: we interrupt succession and so we make weeding work for ourselves. But, and this is well disguised, when we mix plants from different stages of succession these may not blend well, then one or the other is bound to suffer. Thus, the prime example, most trees do not make good companions to vegetables or herbaceous plants. However, there are some plants that may succeed if they come from the same stage of succession. For example, those plants found naturally on the woodland floor, say bluebells, are adapted to niches the trees leave and may succeed where others from sunny glades or meadows may not. So when we jumble plants up it is hardly surprising that some are edged out and others tower above.

Left: Weeds may only be (to some) an eyesore,
as in practice, they're very little competition for an established tree

Understanding plant groups

To be a successful gardener, it really helps to understand how plants have become grouped together in many different ways so we can recreate the conditions and companionships they prefer. As well as the ecological association of different plants by conditions at their origin, they are also connected by their evolution from different families and even from which continent they originated.

Associated by family ancestry and origin, we all, plants and animals together, derive from the most primitive life forms. As evolution proceeded, each line diverged and eventually plants and animals became as we know them now. They are grouped together by their, possibly wrongly divined, ancient connections. Thus, we humans are considered to be a type of primate ape that is related to but not descended from monkeys, and before that from a primitive mammal which itself evolved from a frog-like ancestor, all the way back to the first cell.

Plants are most accurately known by the formation of their flowering parts. (Of course, some groups, such as the ferns, have no flowers – these are usually earlier creations in the evolutionary scale.) 'Modern' plants mostly fall into two series: the Monocotyledons, with single-leaved seeds (lilies, arums, grasses, et al.) and the Dicotyledons, with two-leaved seeds (many annuals and most shrubs, et al.). Seeds are normally the product of pollination and so the flowers, in turn, evolved into forms pollinated by themselves, the wind, and by insects when these arrived on the scene.

Right: Many plants depend on bees for their pollination and, in return, bees rely on flowers for their sustenance

'By their fruits, and, since Linnaeus, by their flowers, ye shall know them.'

Above: Three plants from three families and three continents, strange bedfellows that could never have grown together naturally

So knowing them by the form of their flowers, we refer to the rose family as Rosaceae, the potato/tomato family as Solanaceae or Solanums, and the cabbagey tribe as Brassicas. And, because these are groups of relations, a pest or, more often, a disease that attacks one of the family may well attack another but ignore members from a different family. In other words, cabbage problems may also bother near plant relations such as shepherd's purse or wallflowers, but not bother roses or apples.

Within these families the various ancient flowering forms diverged into sub-groups of closely related plants. These genera are given the Latin names by which we know them, such as Rosa, Pyrus and Malus, for roses, pears and apples. These are all Rosaceae so, along with some few common associations with this family, they also get their more specific ones for their genus. Thus, some apple problems may affect pears and vice versa but each has a whole bunch of their own. And, likewise, they all have their unseen interactions in the soil.

We differentiate each genus into different, though closely related, species. As the original ancient genus prototype adapted to local conditions in slightly different though broadly similar places, so evolved mountain and lowland, wetland and dryland forms, where the background conditions are similar but different enough to be advantageous to distinct variations. When, say, a plant seeding on the wind finds itself evolving in a damper, more humid, but otherwise near identical place from whence it derived, evolution may lose the hairs from its leaves, which will grow more glossy and pointed – all to prevent excess water remaining on and rotting them.

This means it can often be difficult to have a complete collection of many species of one genus in one garden, as each has, for its very existence, evolved under different conditions or associations (such as a different pollinator) to all the other species. Just because of this; different species have different associations with other plants, fungi and creatures in their original ecosystems. So, each species is unlikely to be well served by a generalised average set of conditions, nor by the same companions. Those from the woodland need far different conditions and companions to those from the seashore, and so on. Thus, we have plants that have adapted, by species, from original conditions of high rainfall, low rainfall, frost or not, seaside, mountainside, riverside, bog and woodland to name but a few.

This all boils down to the common sense of growing things that do well in your type of garden; if it's acid soil you must grow acid lovers, for wet soil it must be damp lovers. These may actually be of widely varying genus, but each should be a species that comes from similar places, as these will usually fare better.

Since the earliest life started on one land mass which then split into continents as we know them, there are some ancient plants and associations that exist worldwide, though each continent has developed unique genus and species. Knowing a plant's origin may give us an idea of its individual needs. Thus, we bring together high mountain scree plants under the term Alpines, a group which consisted originally of exactly that but is now composed of those plants that are adapted to such Alpine conditions – all disliking stagnant air or heavy shade and varying more by the type of rock they evolved on than their continent. Those we think of as Mediterranean plants consist of those that like a similar set of conditions to the idealised Mediterranean climate – not just those originating there but also many of the huge number of introductions, especially from the Americas, which are often tender, if not tropical.

A species name may be helpful, if correctly attributed. So we can guess the needs of *alpinum* and *maritimum*, maybe even *sylvaticus*, of woodland, Likewise species from Japan – *japonica*, or more so from Siberia – *kamtschaticum*, are more likely to be hardier than those from Brazil – *brasiliensis* or the Congo, *congolanum*. Beware though, *australis* means southern not Australian. However, it is much easier to be misled by common names: the Jerusalem artichoke is from Canada. While French and African Tagetes marigolds actually come from Central America, as does the Mexican marigold (but this makes up for it with the equally misleading species name of *minuta* - which does not refer to the expected plants' height but the flowers' size, and this is a huge annual, rivalling sunflowers, but with tiny blooms).

One of the inadvertent advantageous effects of our growing 'foreign' plants without their

companions is, say, where the flower has become adapted to a pollinator for which no local substitute exists. In this case, no seed can be set and the blooms may last longer, with even more forming. This is brilliant for bedding displays, but not so good if you want the seed – thus, it may be that runner beans, which can be notoriously difficult to set, do not readily get recognised by native insects.

And, there is another human effect: altering plants. We breed and select what we like, so, just as we ended up with roses, freesias and sweet peas with glorious colours but no scent, we have probably lost many other unnoticed benefits too, such as specific pest or disease resistances or companion interactivity. Breeding to make marigolds less 'pongy' has reduced their ability to discourage pests; so a variety may have a companion effect and another lack it more or less randomly. In one trial of thousands of varieties of oats, just a handful were found to be much more effective at suppressing nearby broad-leaved weeds.

Above: We select those plants we find useful or pretty and take them from their original conditions, often altering them in the process

How we have stuck diverse plants together

Associated through history for our convenience, we have lumped plants into groups to suit the conditions we can create. The ornamental and the productive are kept apart so that each can be given more suitable general conditions, as well as for the obvious aesthetic differences. Vegetables, herbs and soft fruit are artificial groups of diverse plants, though each are generally suited to similar conditions as the other members in each group. Anything not well suited was evicted long ago.

Vegetables are nearly all grown as annuals in sunny open conditions of rich, moist, neutral to slightly alkaline soil. Herbs, often Mediterranean, mostly like sunny, dry, free-draining poor soil and many have silvery leaves (often this colouring is caused by fine hairs which retain humidity in hot conditions but make them prone to rot in the damp). Most soft fruits accept partial shade and enjoy a well-mulched, cool, moist root run, but they are sweeter when their heads are in the sun – all a bit like the sunny glade in which they would be found naturally. So the majority of soft fruits are natural companions, as they (theoretically) could be found growing with one another in such a glade. The orchard fruits have more diverse a history and are grown together with due space and with grass (and preferably companion herbs) underneath merely because that is a convenient way to grow them. (This is also because they compete outrageously if they are grown with other groups, however, to some extent, their greediness can be reduced if the fruits are grafted onto very dwarfing rootstocks.)

It is in the flower garden where we may err most easily, though. Too often we inadvertently end up with mixed borders of almost hostile plantings. It is easier to maintain and succeed with beds devoted to just bedding, or herbaceous perennials or solely to annuals. And, although annuals or even bulbs may succeed temporarily in open spaces between shrubs, these usually soon eliminate all others. Likewise, herbaceous perennials can be mixed with bulbs or the spaces filled with annuals, but add shrubs and soon that's mostly what you'll have unless very dwarfing forms are chosen.

Beware climbers; their nature is to climb and dominate their support, eventually choking it to

Left: This pear has but shallow roots, so benefits from the rhubarb and comfrey's whose deeper roots bring up nutrients from the soil it cannot reach. But, they'd unlikely grow together naturally as they come from different continents

death and bringing it down. Many are far too vigorous for the majority of gardens and, although often beautiful, and usually scented, they cause more than their fair share of problems.

Self-selected weeds are an unnoticed result of our gardening methods; many are nature's way of healing bare soil as, say, when a tree is uprooted, or a landslide or muddy flood occurs. The seed may be extremely long-lived in the ground, waiting for the right moment to germinate or be wind-borne, but either way weeds generally grow fast and seed prolifically. By trying to maintain bare soil or by weeding sporadically and continually creating bare soil, we encourage these weeds and expose ourselves to their attempts at re-colonisation – and we may make it worse by introducing self-seeding garden plants. As the old saying puts it, 'a year's seeds, seven years of weeds' – because weeds are the plants most suited to these conditions, they are also extremely competitive and very bad companions to our chosen plants. Weed control really is needed to minimise the seriously negative companion effects of the soils' rightful heirs.

By creating certain conditions, we inadvertently encourage certain plants to become common weeds amongst our vegetable plots and field crops. By growing only a small number of crop plants for centuries in those beds and fields, these, and those weeds, have evolved a huge number of mutual interactions with each other and also with some pests and diseases. This web is extended further with the systems of predators and parasites moving in to exploit the more concentrated pests and diseases. Unfortunately, this auto control takes place rather too slowly for our needs and we have to try and improve the controls' effectiveness. Choosing suitable companions is, thus, very important for the farmer and for vegetable growers, and so fortunately many interactions have been recorded. By comparison, each flower garden is unique and composed of far more diverse plants, and even different selections of weeds, so far less has been observed or recorded about their interactions. Luckily, by their very diversity (with the notable exception of such ubiquitous plants as roses) the ornamentals are, thus, generally much less afflicted by pests and diseases. They may possibly benefit from companion planting, but other than associating plants found together naturally, this is complicated by their very mixed backgrounds, making them much less predictable.

Right: Sheep's parsley, a common weed, is closely related to carrots and parsnips, and so they all share a common pest; a fly grub that eats their roots

How companion planting works in many subtle ways

As explained on the following pages, there are many different interactions between plants and their environment and, therefore diverse companion effects, all of which may or may not be of use to us. These were categorised by one of the early researchers, Ehrenfried Pfeiffer, who also used crystallisation experiments to determine plant compatibilities. I have expanded his original system into the following ten ways in which these interactions occur, including their companion effects on plants.

Right: The smell of French marigolds makes it harder for pests to find the crops by masking their scents. Its roots are exuding substances to protect it from nematodes and, in doing so, also protects the crops.

1. Plants may be used to aid each other directly

This may be as simple as one supporting another; this happens not only with trees and shrubby climbers but also with sunflowers supporting runner beans and cabbage plants holding up intercrops of French beans. In Classical times, grapevines were trained up elm trees as a preferred prop, indicating some special relationship, as well as simple support.

Plants can also give shelter from the wind or sun. Many tropical crops do better in the shade and, even in the UK summer, salads, spinach and leaf crops can be happier in the light shade of peas or runner beans than in full sun. Japanese maples not only need a suitable leaf-mould-rich soil but require dappled shade and protection from winds too, so they thrive amongst other taller shrubs. Trees and taller plants may break falling rain into a spray, thus saving under-storey plants from a pounding. A hedge breaks the force of a wind but without creating the forceful eddies found with a solid wall. Moreover, when the wind slows down as it passes through the hedge, it converts the energy of motion into warmth and so small fields and gardens bordered by a hedge are significantly warmer, as well as more sheltered, than those with more open boundaries. (This is also because a strong wind makes the apparent temperature of the air lower than the actual. You will notice this yourself; a cold day feels much chillier with a wind blowing.) Many plants stop transpiring and reduce photosynthesis once the wind reaches a speed of more than a few miles an hour, so shelter is crucial for optimum cropping, as well as protection from wind damage. On a smaller scale, this has the same effect when taller crops shelter shorter ones, and even small seedlings benefit from surrounding weeds – if these are not growing too close by.

Right: Runner beans, being legumes, donate nitrates to the sunflowers and can use them for support

Unseen down in the ground, the strong roots of one plant may pierce or crack a soil pan (a compacted impenetrable layer beneath the soil surface) and create channels through which less vigorous roots can follow. Companion plant or just turf roots make a tightly woven mesh and this holds the soil down in one mass, enabling a tree to remain upright despite its own apparently rather small root system. In a bare soil with no companions it might well blow over.

Beneficial root, leaf and gaseous secretions are other important and little-known ways in which plants help each other; they probably intend no such aid but may inadvertently give it when making herbicidal or antibiotic compounds for their own benefit. Some substances are by-products and are simply eliminated when they are of no further use to the owner. However, once discarded these may be valuable to another as a food source, if not for their original purpose.

'Beneficial root, leaf and gaseous secretions are other important and little-known ways in which plants help each other.'

Left: The shady base of a leylandi hedge is hostile to many plants, even most weeds, but this old garden comfrey, *symphytum orientale*, (with an odd honesty and a bluebell) seems immune and flourishes

2. Plants may be used to aid each other indirectly by enriching the soil

Along with the direct effects of secretions used by other plants, there are the indirect value of other by-products as these enrich or improve the soil and, thus, create another sort of benefit. All organic wastes add to the humus content of the soil eventually, so everything that has ever lived has some contribution but some are particularly valuable. All deciduous plants drop their leaves and, along with other plant remains, the leaf-mould formed is extremely good for almost all plants. It not only is a rich source of humus and adds warming darkness to any soil but it is extremely effective at supporting a host of life forms, from small to microscopic and especially the incalculably valuable mycorrhizal fungi. But few spot the petal mould nor the pollen (which is another very rich nutrient source) and these can be found in large amounts. I seldom see the grass through the petals from the cherries – it is a great deal of fresh material to feed the soil at a crucial time in spring. So leave fallen blossoms and leaves on the ground to rot down – the plants may need them more than we can guess.

Seen this way, plants that suffer attacks from hordes of insects are, in fact, creating a richer soil for others from the resultant insect droppings and dead bodies, especially as chitin (insect armour) is very beneficial to soil organisms and plant health.

Some plants are mineral accumulators, collecting scarce elements from the rock particles and from deep down and eventually liberating these through their leaves or, later, from their decaying parts. Only those elements locked up as seeds are lost, and then only temporarily,

Right: Petal fall may add as much fertility as the autumn leaves

for as soon as seeds germinate they can be hoed or pulled out and used as a mulch, so their intrinsic fertility can be released to benefit others. Indeed, seen this way, a flush of weeds well hoed in is like adding a dose of fertiliser.

Green manures are traditional crops grown for their improvement to fertility. They are dug in or composted and used as humus and texture improvers. Most important of these has been the legumes, as their microscopic partners fix nitrogen from the air which is soon available for other plants. (Some other predominantly tropical families have similar benefits but have been little investigated.) Clover is a well-known leguminous companion to grass and has long been included in meadow mixtures, but it is also a benefit in lawns; combining them with grass makes lawns greener and keeps them greener longer in droughts.

Many of the indirect companion effects of plants enriching the soil around them come from the mycorrhizal fungi growing on the roots of different plants. Plants exude unwanted substances into the soil along with acids and substances to help dissolve their prospective foods. The mycorrhizal fungi do a similar job but more effectively, and they exchange their spare nutrients from the plants for carbohydrates, voiding their wastes back into the soil. In turn these wastes feed other lives, which, in turn, liberate other substances, encouraging yet more interactions with even more life forms. One handful of, say, leaf- or petal mould does not just feed the plants directly but also feeds soil organisms, then the mycorrhizal fungi, and then the plants again, increasing in quantity and value at each stage as it becomes yet more wastes and dead cells.

One of the least-known effects is how poor soils encourage fungi that protect themselves with antibiotics, which are then taken up by the plants. It is ironic how we test animal products for antibiotic residues but not crops – as we do not apply antibiotics to plants, there seems no point – but as plants absorb antibiotics from soils, and more antibiotics are produced in worked-out soils, then some modern field crops may carry a hidden danger.

Left: Clovers are leguminous, enrich the soil which feeds the nitrogen-hungry grasses and so produces greener lusher swards

3. Plants to be avoided, or even combined, which oppose or harm each other

As explained on page 70 with rose replant disease, the worst plant to follow another in its space in the soil is the same one as before, and likewise the worst companion may be more of the same, as these would compete for identical resources.

All plants are in competition for air, light, water and nutrients, and so theoretically, they would all do better on their own. However, there are some combinations that really do not get on more than simple competition would indicate; this is probably because a root, leaf or gaseous secretion given off by one is hostile to the other or to its mycorrhizal fungi. Certainly, dandelions give off ethylene, which prevents seeds germinating and alters their growth and ripening (though we can turn this to our advantage, as dandelion leaves or bananas can help ripen reluctant tomatoes). Many plants give off allelopathic, herbicidal, compounds to ensure their own weed control, especially those such as pines, glossy evergreens, aromatic herbs and heathers, which can all be bad companions for anything to be sown in situ and may also adversely affect some mature plants. So, although these may be useful as barrier hedges to vegetable plots, they should not be grown within the beds, as these allelopathic substances will spoil seed germination and possibly also damage yields. Within the plot it's well worth observing that onions hate beans and vice versa, and peppers hate radishes, so keep these enemies apart. Couch grass, *Agropyron repens*, is a tough weed but it can be suppressed by growing tomatoes, rape and *Tagetes minuta*. Pittosporum is considered a bad companion to many, rue likewise, and little gets on with wormwood. Some flowers, Shasta daisies for example, when cut and placed in a vase with others will cause them to wilt. It is also thought that pines are bad trees to have around your compost heap, whereas elderberry or birch are good as they aid the composting process.

Left: Dandelions give off ethylene gas which suppresses germination, alters growth and speeds ripening - not often a good companion

4. Plants where a small ratio of one aids the growth of another, though a larger percentage hinders or harms

The probability here is that, initially, one plant is providing a secretion or waste that encourages a mycorrhizal partner of the other, but then if the ratio rises this is offset by the more straightforward competition effect. For obvious reasons, these effects have been noticed most by farmers. Corn weeds, such as corn cockles, cornflowers and poppies, and especially the wild corn marigolds and chamomiles, are alleged to encourage a better corn crop if just a few of them are present, but they will ruin it if they grow in quantity. Chamomile is said to be the plant physician that will aid those put near it and is an interesting, if much misidentified, plant. The much-loathed stinging nettle is another plant that seems to have beneficial effects, especially on storing abilities, if grown near crops but it soon overwhelms and chokes them if it is uncontrolled. Yarrow in moderation stimulates oil production in aromatic herbs; germination, seed formation and vigour in many plants improves when sown with coriander, but not the cabbage family, and birch trees planted in moderation will improve the growth of larches. The foxglove is also reputed to affect those near it – and considering the potency of its drug and its effect on mammalian hearts, it may well have some interesting exudates and wastes.

Right: A bed of raspberries and asparagus (yes I know it's unusual but think about it) finds little competition and much benefit from the deeper rooting salsify and the sulphurous allium Rocamboles

5. Plants used to repel pests

Many plant combinations mask each other with scent (or leaf form and colour) and so confuse pests hunting their prey, but some are not just camouflage but are also able to repel pests. It's widely accepted that the smelly pong of French marigolds, Tagetes, is effective against whitefly, as these will not enter a greenhouse with marigolds within. However, the smell is not so strong as to drive them out if they're carried in on a plant. (So exercise rigorous quarantine controls on your imports.) The Shoofly plant, *Nicandra physaloides*, is also reckoned to stop whitefly coming in, but it grows so big that it almost excludes them physically and so is less practical. All Tagetes marigolds are good companions outdoors as well, where their smell confuses pests, though some are still attractive to butterflies and bees. Garlic and other Alliums are strong smelling and have often been used as companions to keep off pests generally. More specifically, trailing nasturtiums repel woolly aphids, which are said to disappear from apple trees after the third year. Cabbage white caterpillars are strongly repelled by bugle (*Ajuga reptans*) extract, though admittedly the plant itself has less effect. Slugs are repelled by extracts of herb Robert, soapwort, marjoram and ginger and will not cross crushed horse chestnuts or crushed *Cyclamen purpurascens*.

'Pests may be not only confused by smelly plants but some so shun certain scents these may be used to repel them - curiously, the smell of garlic is reckoned sufficient to deter even a vampire...'

Right: French marigolds (Tagetes), are exceptionally good pest-repelling plants and especially effective at keeping whitefly out of greenhouses

6. Plants used to attract, trap or destroy pests

Obviously, some plants are more attractive to certain pests than others, so slugs will leave your hostas alone if you plant Chinese cabbage or lettuce nearby or scatter their leaves around; these plants are grown as sacrificials in this situation, to attract the pest away, and are intended to suffer. The sacrificial plant may be of another genus, species or even just another variety. It has been investigated how birds prefer one apple variety to another by the number of fruits damaged, but isn't it obvious they would have a preference. Another excellent example is with autumn-sown onions; the slugs much prefer 'Buffalo' to any other variety so, by mixing this in with others they are left alone, indeed effectively thinned by the slugs munching on the 'Buffalo'. Likewise, growing a slug-prone variety such as 'Cara' or 'Picasso' potatoes in amongst your 'prize' crop will keep those cleaner. Blackberries in the perimeter hedges save grapes (well, a few of them) from the birds.

Sacrificials may first attract away a pest, thus saving the plant, but they may also control other pests on your protected plants by concentrating the pests and enabling a parasite or predator to then increase in numbers and destroy the pests. Of course, the best predator can be us; in this way we get trap plants, and so, having been lured to them, the pests can then be eliminated. If you simply plant Chinese cabbage next to your hostas, they will not just attract away the slugs but go on to breed them up. So the plants can be taken away before that happens, complete with slugs, and composted and more grown in their place. (Though save clean leaves as more bait for elsewhere in the garden.) This process of placing trap plants amongst the protected plants is effective for reducing numbers but it can never eliminate all of them. Still, enough are removed to make control by other measures more likely. So, if your

Left: Sprouted potato tubers placed on grapevines attract mealy bugs onto themselves for collection and dispatch

greenhouse plants are infested with whitefly, interspersing pots of nicotiana will lure many over. A quick spray with sugar solution will stick the whiteflies down and the plants can go off to the compost with them. After another batch of nicotiana, more of the flies are gone. Obviously repetition is necessary, but then it does work significantly well. Red spider mite cannot resist broad beans so, again, pot-grown ones mixed amongst infested plants, lure them on board and they can be carried away. As these mites climb upwards it's best to stand the bean pots on top of other pots to get their heads just above, but still touching, the infested plants.

Mealy bug are lured onto sprouting potato tubers hung on grapevines, or onto tomato plants in pots. Sprouting damaged (for the smell) potatoes loosely buried near potato plants or carrots will lure the slugs and wireworms onto themselves so these can be picked off with a weekly inspection.

Some plants harbour pests underneath, making them easy to find. Alpine strawberries make useful companions anyway but on the vegetable bed they are sure to have some slugs and millipedes, wood lice and other pests hiding within their dry insides – which can be easily inspected and tidied! Miner's lettuce (*Claytonia perfoliata*) is a winter salad plant that turns pinkish when slugs are nibbling underneath – a dead giveaway. Lift the pinkish leaves away and there are the pests to dispatch.

Other plants even do the work for us. *Solanum sisymbriifolium*, a weird tomato relative, is a prickly species whose root exudates cause potato eelworm cysts to burst into growth but then it starves the nematodes who can't feed on its roots. Likewise, infestations of root knot nematodes decrease where leaves of Madagascar primrose (*Caltharanthus roseus*) are incorporated. Tagetes marigolds give off nematode-killing secretions and Crotalaria, castor oil plants, *Calendula officinalis*, sage, asparagus, petunias and dahlias all hinder some varieties of eelworm. Slugs and snails were killed by an extract from *Euphorbia splendens* so it may be assumed a barrier of this would be very effective.

Right: This tomato relative, *Solanum sisymbriifolum*, can restore land
no longer fit for potatoes from eelworm infestation

7. Plants used to attract and sustain beneficial 'bugs'

Obviously, including plants in your garden that bring in more predators, parasites and pollinators is a good thing. There is a dearth of information on specific attractants and, ironically, some of the best plants for this sort of insect encouragement are weeds. These have some immediate objections but nonetheless are very effective. Hogweed (*Heracleum sphondylium*) flowers have been recorded as visited by 118 species of insect! (See Appendix II on page 104 for weeds with high attractant value.)

Many garden flowers have good all-round appeal: *Limnanthes douglasii*, *Phacelia tanacetifolia*, *Convolvulus tricolor*, buckwheat and crimson clover are especially valuable. Generally it helps to provide as much variety of flowers as is feasible, and from early in the year. Avoid highly bred varieties and double-flowered sorts as these may have little value.

Bugs don't just need nectar and pollen for food, though this serves many adults, but some need meat as well. Thus, it pays to have pest bankers, sacrificial plants that are grown to suffer the pests which will feed increasing numbers of control agents for other plants (see page 53 – sacrificial plants). Honeysuckles, sweet cherries and redcurrants all suffer huge aphid attacks to little real detriment and go on to raise an army of predators, such as ladybirds and lacewings.

Other plants can provide water, such as lupins and lady's mantle (*Alchemilla mollis*) by keeping drops nestling in their leaves. Teasels are especially good as they store little pools in their stem joints. Old conifers, evergreens and dense hedges are often good for providing shelter, nest and hibernation sites. Long rough grass, small bushy perennials and bramble thickets are also very useful and enable bigger populations to survive and overwinter. Most useful of all, though, is probably ivy which covers trees and walls with dense mats of dry hiding places and flowers late with copious pollen and nectar.

In fact, every garden needs a wide range of diverse habitats to provide for micro-fauna, and the more variety we can create the better. Areas of weeds are immensely valuable, rough grass is said to liberate a ground beetle from every square foot which can venture out to eat pests and their eggs. Ground covered with dense plants, rather than bare soil, is preferable and over winter green manures or other cover crops act as insect preserves where bare soil would be almost sterile. Even flushes of weeds are thus seen as useful.

Above: Old wood with a mossy coat provides a comfy home for ladybirds

8. Plants useful for attracting birds

Although often a problem for fruit and with seedlings and seed crops, birds are such a huge help with pest control that they do need encouraging. Just one family of tits or robins will consume tens of thousands of caterpillars and other grubs. Thrushes are well known for eating snails, first bashing them to bits on their anvils (usefully placed big stones), and even the b***** blackbirds do a lot of good. And they all drop fertility everywhere they go.

To encourage birds, first keep cats contentedly indoors then provide the birds with food, especially in winter, with a bird table augmented with berrying shrubs and seeding plants – especially grasses and those with oily seeds such as sunflowers, milk thistle, *Silybum marianum* and flax. Then plant dense shrubs for nest sites – it helps to bend and tie supple branches into tripods, creating crotches in which nests can be lodged. As there is a shortage of natural nesting materials, plant bulrushes, pampas grass, globe artichokes and cardoons and other fluff-producing plants. Of course, more nesting holes and perching places will help, so don't cut down old trees, just make them safe. Do not forget that birds need water, so plant more teasels for their stem-joint pools (see page 56), and do have a bird bath!

Birds are obviously fond of fruit – I don't need to tell gardeners that – but as noted previously, they do have preferences and they peck apples and pears selectively, thus 'Lord Lambourne' and 'Cox's Orange Pippin' are much more heavily damaged than 'Laxton's Fortune' and 'Worcester Pearmain', and 'Conference' pears are four times as much damaged as 'Williams''. If you want really happy birds, plant redcurrants, tayberries and grapes.

Left: A bird bath is a valuable aid; it not only washes and waters the bird population generally - but also refreshes thirsty birds, saving them eating even more fruit

9. Plants used to repel animal pests

Hedges, barriers, prickles and thorns are all mainstays of gardens plagued with unwanted four- and two-legged visitors. Quickthorn, hawthorn or crataegus is one of the best and most easily maintained; Pyracantha and berberis offer more scenic options; while holly has a cash value come December and is probably the best choice. In warmer areas, *Poncirus trifoliata* is a slow-growing but extremely architectural and sweetly scented relative of citrus that has staggeringly deterrent thorns. The blackberry tribe make forbidding barriers to bigger animals, either as mounds or trained on wires, but allow smaller ones through easily. The hybrid berries, such as loganberry, have more, much smaller thorns that are just as unpleasant. A bed of yuccas, Spanish bayonet or just roses will stop most intruders.

Smells can be effective deterrents. Stinking mayweed (*Anthemis cotula*) has a vile odour that can be used to repel rodents and fleas. (Also effective against fleas are rue, mint and catnip, Nepeta.) Dwarf elder (*Sambucus ebulus*) has a foetid vanilla-like smell, and leaves placed in seed boxes deter mice, or mix narcissi, scilla and muscari with your tulips to protect them from mice. Mice also dislike the camphor plant, most euphorbias, wormwood, corn chamomile and the everlasting pea (*Lathyrus latifolius*). In trials, mice showed most distaste for cinnamon, pepper, pine needles and extract of rhubarb root.

Several strongly pongy plants, including euphorbias, castor oil, chives and incarvillea, have been said to repel moles, so try them. However, be warned that success consistently eludes most attempts.

Right: Thorns are better deterrents than signs. This is *Poncirus trifoliata*, a hardy citrus relative - also bears gorgeous scented white blooms and odd furry musky, theoretically edible, oranges

10. Plants used to repel or reduce fungal and other diseases

It is asserted that chives and garlic make roses less prone to blackspot and mildews; this is an area possibly confused with companions that improve general vigour and resistance. Unfortunately, it is hard to tell the difference, however, nature does give examples: Eucryphia trees support a benign fungus, Gliocladium, and this produces volatile compounds which then control Pythium and Verticillium diseases. Thus eucryphias inadvertently protect other plants nearby.

Coatings of yeasts and other micro-organisms also protect against diseases and these may be encouraged by pollen or exudations from other plants. It is reckoned that the mere presence of some, such as chamomile, stinging nettles and especially the alliums, may give nearby plants some protection, but it seems their extracts are much more potent. And using sprays, no matter how useful, is not really companion planting. Still, if the spray works then the plant itself may well help a tad. Chive sprays have been used against downy and powdery mildew on cucumbers and gooseberries; leaf extracts of Japanese knotweed, Fallopia (*Reynoutria japonica*) controls powdery mildew infestations on many crop plants; Kiwi fruits contain a protein that checks botrytis and grey mould, as do extracts of cauliflower leaves and oils extracted from thyme and oregano; and horseradish tea has likewise been used against brown rot in apples. Significantly, both the presence and extracts of peppermint, summer savory and thyme reduce infestations of clubroot disease amongst brassicas, whereas the traditional remedy of rhubarb has but little effect.

Right: Rocambole garlic, a pungent allium, grown in quantity here, helps prevent fungal attacks on nearby fruit trees and to this new raspberry bed

Applying companion effects to our advantage — and a few complications

The challenge for companion gardeners is, firstly, our lack of precise information of these many plant interactions and, secondly, the sheer diversity and interplay of these effects. There are conflicting and abetting, direct and indirect, negative and positive effects. A tree may help a plant underneath it with leaf and petal litter, sustain predators of the plant's main pests, break the force of the wind and heavy rain, create suitable dappled shade and exude beneficial secretions, yet simply choke the plant out with increasing shade or by competing for soil moisture. Wormwood most certainly discourages butterflies from laying their eggs on cabbages but, at the same time, the cabbages dislike the wormwood so much that their yield drops significantly.

Right: Fallen petals may have a profound effect; altering soil fertility and promoting or hindering certain micro-organisms, just as may fallen leaves

Our skill is to find the interactions we can introduce to help us, but also not to put known bad companions near each other. And this last facet cannot be overstressed; this is an important area of knowledge that is not well researched, so we could probably benefit more from knowing which plants do not get on than from knowing more about those that do.

Interplanting and intercropping for simple gains

Companion planting is, thus, complicated by the interplay of many interactions. Some plants may be only little altered by the presence of some other, save for straightforward competition for water, nutrients et al., however, there is still an advantage to be gained by simple interplanting. Doubling the numbers of the same plant in the same space would mean they compete for exactly the same resources, but mix in the same number of a different plant and these may compete less. This is excellent and long-established practice, particularly for adding leguminous plants. So, if you have three fields, in each you grow one of three crops and you will get a given harvest of all three; now in exchange for more labour you interplant all three crops in all three fields and the total yield is now greater. In agriculture, this method produces gains of 20 per cent or so when beans are mixed with cereals, or even certain cereals with other, different cereals. Some crops may gain companion benefits on top, too – sweet corn with dwarf French beans and squashes is a classic combination. Planting dwarf French beans and cabbages together also works well against their pests, and mixing brassicas with clover or bird's foot trefoil reduces aphid attacks and maintains yields. Broad beans significantly help main-crop potatoes, making this another productive combination.

Right: Nasturtiums grow well with sweet corn

Pre-companions and companion effects over time

It is generally considered that companion planting is about growing two or more plants together for the benefits this brings to one, the other, or both. However, there are other effects that occur over time that are just as important and need to be considered when you are deciding what to plant, when and where.

As explained earlier, there is a natural succession of plants on a site. From the initial colonisers of bare rock, thereafter the early inhabitants are superseded by other plants of increasing size and durability, through herbaceous to, usually, shrubs, then trees. Thus, at any stage, the soil is most able to support certain groups of plants more than others. Trees will seldom succeed on bare weathered rock, for the extreme example, but at any given time the state of the soil will equally determine the likely success of other plants.

You need a rich, moist, friable soil for many of our choicer garden plants, especially the highly bred ones, such as vegetables, but natural colonisers, such as 'wild flowers', are mostly in need of poorer soil. Given rich soil these plants grow rank and are soon overcome by other, better adapted, plants. So if you want to establish such colonisers in an area it's necessary to strip off the top layer of soil to expose the poorer stuff underneath. This will suit the colonisers and disadvantage their competitors that are more suited to rich soil, such as grasses. A similar situation is a sour wet soil – in nature this would probably be a peat bog, thus you are likely to be continually fighting mosses, liverworts, rushes and other plants found in such places. Rather than struggling to change the soil conditions you may do better choosing

natural succession plants, such as blueberries or cranberries, which are well adapted to such conditions and which will fill the niche and have a chance of doing well despite the 'weeds'.

Another factor to consider is how some plants change their soil conditions to their own detriment in the short run but for a longer-term advantage. If any sort of plant continues to occupy the soil for a long time it slowly changes the conditions, making itself unsuitable for them, and this is compounded by pests and diseases building up to high levels. So if the plant was to disappear for some time the soil could recover and the pests and diseases die away. Thus, we find that many plants, once they have been in a spot for a while, die away only to return later when well advantaged once more.

This is probably due to the allelopathic ('herbicidal') substances given off by the roots or leaves. The classic example is clover sickness when, after a period under clover, the plants

Above: Blueberries combine well with wild strawberries or cranberries rambling underneath

become weak and succumb to fungal or eelworm infections. Clover seed will then not germinate on that spot for some time because the parents gave off secretions that stop their seed germinating, even when diluted to three hundred parts per million. However, soon these substances are broken down and then clover can germinate and regrow.

Rice sickness is similar, while the last crops' residues are rotting down new plants are prevented from establishing by chemicals that are given off. Only once these are gone can new plants succeed. Farmers have learnt to work around this, so whilst the residues break down, they start off new plants in a special area then transplant these when the paddy field is ready again.

Another reason for such apparently suicidal behaviour is because of the difficulty of distributing seeds afar; unfortunately most drop very close by! An existing perennial plant does not want its own offspring any more than it wants weeds growing up all around it and choking it, so when finding themselves underneath the parent or similar, their seeds are suppressed as well as those of weeds. But if the parent dies, soon the allelopathic compounds have gone and the seeds are able to germinate into the gap. Some trees, such as the American black walnut (*Juglans nigra*) are able to prevent almost all seeds germinating underneath them. Knapweeds (centaurea) and Marsh marigolds (*Caltha palustris*) have very powerful allelopathic exudates which inhibit other plants' seeds from germinating. Likewise, pine woods, lavender beds and most shiny leaved evergreens create a soil in which seeds have difficulty germinating and often even transplants have trouble rooting.

So trying to sow or plant a new plant in the same place where one of the same has just been is often difficult. This is known as the replant problem – the most commonly occurring form being rose (replant) sickness. This is not a disease but the symptomatic poor growth of another rose where one has previously grown. Given time, this slowly disappears and a rose can be established again. However, the rest time needed can be shortened by adding huge quantities of fertiliser, compost or a mix of suitable micro-organisms to the soil – any of these eliminate or counteract whatever it is that is preventing the new rose getting away. The same applies to almost every other plant to some degree, and is not just a problem with trees and shrubs.

Right: Plants such as wild geraniums soon colonise bare ground

Rotations

To overcome such residual problems which are worsened by the repetitive cropping in the vegetable bed, we adopt what are called rotations. Essentially, this means that the same crop is not returned to the same spot for as long as feasible; in practice, this usually means a three- or four-year rotation. For example, first peas and beans with a dressing of lime, followed by the brassicas or sweet corn and squashes with a dressing of well-rotted compost or manure, then root crops or alliums and, finally potatoes and tomatoes with another dressing of well-rotted compost or manure.

Most rotations have been developed pragmatically; the lime which is needed to keep the soil sweet (slightly alkaline for most vegetables) is added with the peas and beans who, being leguminous, need it, as do the brassicas which follow, and the lime is kept well away from the potatoes, who get more scab in limey soils. The well-rotted manure or compost is given to the hungry feeders (brassicas, potatoes, tomatoes and sweet corn) who appreciate it most and after the peas and beans (which do not need it) and sufficiently before the roots (which will fork if given fresh stuff). Also this keeps the compost or manure away from the lime, because if they are added together they interact, losing value.

The gap of at least three years before a crop returns enables the soil to become suitable for each specific crop once again, any pests and diseases are handicapped, allelopathic self-seed suppressants break down and the three alternate crops' residues repair the fertility. Even weeds are disadvantaged, as those suited to hiding amongst peas or beans struggle when they are exposed by, say, sweet corn. The continually changing conditions make it harder for most weeds to succeed. (Indeed, the most generally successful weeds are those quickest to seed, and these are selected for by poor weeding repeated too infrequently – if just a few escape they reproduce and multiply outrageously.)

However, although it seems probable that such a general plan of rotation makes sense, it may not be the optimum approach. It is likely that in any given soil some crops may well do better for another reason – depending on the previous crop. Certainly the brassicas benefit from the rich soil created by the rotting leguminous roots, but do the potatoes prefer the soil left by the roots (which is, of course, also broken up) or by the alliums (either of which precede them in this rotation)? Such interactions over time are even less known about than immediate companion interactions, yet we already utilise these pre-companion effects in two ways: with green manures and clearance crops.

Above: We can't expect companion plants to overcome problems unless we also employ simple basic measures, such as crop rotation

Green manures

These are 'pre-companions', in that we benefit the plants that follow by deliberately growing fertility-enhancing crops on the site, then incorporating them into the soil before the chosen crop is sown. Traditionally this method comes from agriculture, so we find the leguminous plants most often employed are clover, tares and vetches, field beans and lupins, but also humus-creators such as Hungarian grazing rye. Sadly, although effective, most of these are more suited to those with tractors and ploughs and are pernicious weeds to the gardener; they're just too hard to dig in or cart away to compost and return. They can be killed off, though, by covering them with opaque plastic or groundcovering fabric for a month or two.

Whether smothered or dug in, these green manures take up to two months or so to break down sufficiently for the crop to succeed. However, other more garden-worthy green manures are miner's lettuce (*Claytonia perfoliata*), lamb's lettuce, (*Valerianella*), borage, and the poached-egg plant (*Limnanthes douglasii*). All these are quicker and easier to kill or strip off and give dense weed-suppressing growth through winter. In addition, the first pair also make good eating.

Right: A novel green manure I'm experimenting with is this beautiful golden comfrey, which does not persist as does the usual

Mineral accumulators

Mineral accumulators are plants known to be good at accumulating certain minerals – which are often those that are in short supply, thus making these very competitive plants that are not good for mixing in with crops or valuable ornamental displays. However, if grown as a green manure beforehand they accumulate the mineral in short supply then, when they are composted or dug in before their seed has set, this mineral becomes more available as their remains decay and rot away. Ironically, many weeds are superb mineral accumulators, which is one reason why they are so much of a problem, but as many are winter hardy they can, in fact, be one of the best of the green manures – and free! The important point is that they must be killed before they set seed and only those that do not create other problems should be encouraged (not plants such as groundsel, which harbours clubroot, for instance). A list of the weeds with most potential is given in Appendix IV on page 110.

Right: Ground elder is the worst sort of weed; quick to establish and hard to eradicate - yet rich in minerals and feeding more than a hundred insects with its flowers

Clearance crops

These also have a hugely important pre-companion effect. As plant residues decay in the soil, they release substances that kill or encourage soil micro-organisms, altering the soil populations and, thus, making it more or less suitable for the crops that follow. As mentioned on page 54, *Solanum sisymbriifolium* is a thorny tomato relative which, when grown on a soil, encourages the eelworm cysts of the pathological nematodes to burst into life, expecting their prey of a potato crop to now be available. Instead, finding that these plants do not succour them they die away, leaving the soil cleaner and ready for potatoes once more. Likewise, though not as efficiently so they need multiple courses, short-term stands of mustard can reduce clubroot infestations, allowing crops of brassicas to succeed again. Soya beans dug in before planting strawberries reduces their root rots, and soya beans incorporated before potatoes will reduce scab. Of course, this may all be due to physical effects, such as making the soil more acidic, with more humus or of a better tilth. A prior crop of flax or spinach will leave fibrous and saponin-like compounds which improve the crumb structure and so these are beneficial to many crops.

'Perhaps the greatest advance will be when we find crops which best precede others.'

Left: Spinach is a good green manure and clearance crop unrelated to most and enriching the soil

Specific companionships well worth employing or avoiding in the vegetable bed

(see Appendix I for a summary)

Although not replacing good gardening methods, it is worth trying to ensure that vegetables, which are tricky, highly bred plants, are given only their best companions nearby and never planted near or next to crops they do not get on with. Interplanting may not be necessary, but certainly try to avoid having bad companions in adjacent rows.

Allium family

Garlic is the most pungent and most effective accumulator of sulphur, which may explain its very ancient reputation as a fungicide. Garlic emulsion kills aphids and onion flies and is also used against codling moths, snails, root maggots, Japanese beetles, carrot root fly and peach leaf curl. Garlic is especially good for roses and fruit trees and works well with vetch. Keep garlic away from beans and peas, though they may follow in rotation.

Garlic does not go well with
legumes, except in cassoulet

Onions; the mutual detestation with beans is well known; peas do not grow well with onions either. Brassicas, beet, tomatoes and lettuce grow well with onions, as do strawberries. Summer savory may be beneficial to onions, chamomile aids onions when in small amounts, and carrots or leeks are often intercropped so that the onion flies and carrot flies are confused, and onion extracts have proved efficacious at preventing hatching of many insect eggs. When the onions are swelling and ripening it's beneficial to let weeds grow to take up spare moisture and nutrients, particularly nitrogen, so the bulbs then keep better.

Leeks are not so miserable with beans as onions and go well with celery and carrots. Leeks decrease attacks of carrot root flies and hide brassicas from pigeons, but they may not get on well with broccoli.

Shallots also do not get on with peas and beans. Plantains harbour shallot aphids (*Myzus ascalonius*); insect pests which also attack strawberries.

Asparagus grows well with tomatoes; asparagus leaf extracts protect the vegetable from its beetle while its root secretions kill *Trichodorus*, a nematode that attacks tomato roots. As both like basil, these three make a happy trio. Parsley does well with asparagus, but only if the soil is moist. Potatoes also grow well with asparagus, though they are hard to extract without damaging its roots. Onions and other alliums are disliked by asparagus.

Amaranth is beneficial to both maize and onions and also acts as a host plant to ground beetles which control many pests by eating their eggs.

Beet and chards do well with most beans, though not with runners. They like lettuce, onions and brassicas, especially kohlrabi. However, brassica-related weeds, such as charlock and wild mustard, are particularly detrimental. Beets prevent corn cockle seeds germinating, though these are rarely a problem in gardens.

Right: Do not grow beet in the shade
of runner beans

'Avoiding bad companions is more important than putting good ones together.'

Brassicas

The cabbage family benefit from herbs, such as chamomile, dill, peppermint, rosemary and sage. They do well with peas, celery, potatoes, onions and dwarf beans but not with rue, runner beans, lettuce or strawberries. Tomatoes are controversial; they may aid spring cabbage though, in the UK, the spring cabbages are often eaten before the tomatoes are planted! Tomatoes can attract cabbage butterflies from brassicas and deter flea beetles, but they hinder broccoli and are themselves severely inhibited.

Brassicas are all prone to clubroot disease, however, exudates from peppermint, summer savory and thyme significantly reduce infestations. Planting bits of rhubarb stalks with them has been shown to have only a small beneficial effect. Undersowing brassicas with clover or bird's foot trefoil reduces aphid infestations without harming yields. Cabbage white caterpillars are most discouraged by the taste of bugle (*Ajuga reptans*) extract. Interplanting brassicas with French beans significantly reduces pest levels on both.

Trials show that, although you could follow a broccoli crop with a cabbage crop successfully, you couldn't follow it with cauliflowers, due to inhibitory substances from the broccoli roots. Sawdust, even just one per cent, added to soils makes brassica seedlings more likely to succumb to Pythium, which causes damping off.

Kohlrabi is another slightly different brassica; it does not get on with tomatoes, strawberries, peppers or runner beans, but does with onions, beet and cucumber.

Turnips are another member of the cabbage family that share their general traits; they get on very well with peas and are benefited by vetches, especially hairy tare (*Vicia hirsute*), keeping off aphids. They do not like hedge mustard and knotweeds.

Chinese greens, cabbage or pak choi are brassicas close to mustard that grow well with Brussels sprouts. In the USA these are used as sacrificial plants for maize crops as they attract their corn worms.

Right: Carrots are not just a good crop but, if left to flower, superb for beneficial insects

Carrots left to flower attract hoverflies and beneficial wasps and have been recorded as visited by 61 species of insect. Plagued by their carrot root fly, numerous herbs and strong-smelling remedies have been used with some success, mostly from onions, leeks and salsify. Carrots' general health is better when planted near chives, celery, lettuce, radish and tomatoes. They promote growth in peas but dislike anise and dill, although the latter helps discourage their root fly. Carrots stored near apples may acquire a bitter taint. On the farm, heavy soil may be improved the year before sowing them by digging in a green manure of flax or soya beans.

Celery does well with beans, tomatoes and leeks, and benefits brassicas by deterring cabbage white butterflies. If left to flower, celery will attract many beneficial insects, especially predatory wasps. Celery rust can be prevented with nettles and equisetum tea sprayed on their leaves.

Celeriac will do well with most brassicas, leeks, onions and tomatoes. It grows best following legumes, especially after a green manure of vetch and between rows of runner beans.

Cucurbits

Outdoor or Ridge cucumbers need pollination and do well under maize or sunflowers in the light shade. They like dill, peas and beans, beet and carrots, but mutually dislike potatoes and most strong herbs, especially sage. Cucumbers may attract whitefly from tomatoes but tomato root exudates inhibit cucumber plants so these should never be planted together. Stinging nettle tea may prevent cucumbers getting downy mildew, and extracts of garlic and field horsetail control their powdery mildew.

Winter squashes and pumpkins may grow healthier with a few datura weeds and will do well under sweet corn but they do not like potatoes.

Marrows, courgettes/zucchini and summer squashes. These grow well with sweet corn, peas and beans but should avoid potatoes. Rue is bad for courgettes.

Jerusalem artichokes will suppress ground elder and horsetail (equisetum).

Legumes

Broad beans suffer from black aphid infestations which spend the winter on the wild spindle tree (*Euonymas europaeus*) or on fat hen or black nightshade and may also attack beetroot and spinach. Black aphids are discouraged by summer savory planted nearby. Broad beans are mutually beneficial with potatoes and discourage gooseberry sawfly caterpillars.

Left: I find squashes combine well with nasturtiums

Dwarf, French or haricot beans do well with celery and produce earlier crops with strawberries, which themselves benefit from the association. Parsley and parsnip seeds contain antibiotics that protect beans from botrytis. Interplanting French beans with brassicas significantly reduces pest levels on both.

Peas do well with roots, beans, celeriac, potatoes, cucurbits and sweet corn, and with most herbs if they do not create too much shade. They do not like most alliums, though leeks are tolerated. Gladioli are supposed not to like peas. Root exudates from peas increase the availability of many elements. Pea powdery mildew is controlled by ginger or sweet flag extracts which also stimulate vigour if sprayed on well diluted.

Runner beans are inhibited by onions and have the same affinities as other beans. They dislike kohlrabi and sunflowers but grow well with sweet corn, also protecting it from corn army worms. Runner beans get on with most brassicas, especially Brussels sprouts, and may beneficially shade celery and salads in hot weather.

Lettuces do best amongst cucumbers, carrots, radishes and strawberries and may not prosper near broccoli. Tomato root exudates inhibit and suppress lettuces. Lettuces can be protected from aphids with chervil. If the weather is hot, sow seeds in the shade as they will not germinate above 18°C (65°F). Lettuce is one of the plants that has been shown to take up natural antibiotics from the soil. Rue prevents lettuce seeds from germinating. Poplars nearby increase risk of root aphids on lettuce, which overwinter on these trees.

Parsnips grow well with lettuce and with peas, if not shaded too much by them. Parsnip seeds contain antibiotics that protect them against botrytis, and liquid extracts of parsnips have proved protective to French beans. The flowers attract hoverflies and predatory wasps and make a sacrificial crop for carrot blossom moths.

Radishes benefit from nasturtium and mustard, and chervil, lettuce and peas will all get on well together with them. Radishes detest hyssop, do not like grapes and spinach and are not liked by peppers. Tomato root exudates suppress radishes.

Right: Carrots can be sown with radish which, when pulled, provide the slower growing carrots more space

Solanums

Keep potatoes, tobacco, peppers, aubergines and tomatoes well away from each other as they have many common problems.

Potatoes do not get on with cabbages. Horseradish aids potatoes but must be carefully contained; peas help them considerably. Tagetes marigolds are beneficial, as are celery, flax, lamium, nasturtium and summer savory. Potatoes are mutually beneficial with beans and maize. Sunflowers, cucurbits, orache, many trees and raspberries are not good for potatoes. Potato eelworm is harboured by black and woody nightshade; Tagetes will kill many eelworms, as will green manures of mustard, barley or oats or especially of *Solanum sisymbriifolium* grown beforehand. Onions and other alliums going before prevent Rhizoctonia infections. Scab can be avoided by putting grass clippings or comfrey leaves in with potato sets and reduced by digging in soya bean plants beforehand. Potatoes are spoiled and tainted easily in store by strong odours and ripening or rotting fruits. Cold extracted juice from sprouted tubers is extremely toxic to bacteria and may prove useful at preventing rots.

Tomato root exudates inhibit cucumbers so these should never be planted together, and more usefully inhibit couch grass while other exudates from tomato leaves suppress radishes and lettuce. Rue prevents tomato seeds from germinating. Like most plants, tomatoes loathe fennel, wormwood and dislike all brassicas, especially kohlrabi. However, bits of tomato leaf do repel flea beetles. Tomatoes get on well with basil, alliums, marigolds and nasturtiums and the fruits store longer if they were grown near nettles. Some varieties agree with parsley while others disagree with it. Tomatoes do particularly well with asparagus. Tomato leaf spray has been used against asparagus beetles and the asparagus roots kill *Trichodorus*, a nematode that attacks tomatoes. *Tagetes erecta* grown with tomatoes protects them from nematodes and the soil fungal disease *Alternaria solani*. A strange but effective combination is tomatoes with roses, as they protect the plant from blackspot. They may inhibit apricot seedlings and may be protective to gooseberries. Interestingly, they have been shown to take up antibiotics from the soil.

Spinach grows well with strawberries but dislikes cauliflower and radishes.

Sunflower blooms are good for bees, lacewings and predatory wasps.

Sunflower plants are hungry feeders though, and inhibit many plants, especially potatoes, runner beans and grass. They are inhibited from germinating themselves by grass and do not get on with sweet corn. Cucurbits grow well underneath them.

Sweet corn (maize) does well with beans and particularly well with peas. Their light shade makes them friendly to cucumbers, melons, squashes, courgettes, marrows and even to potatoes. Tomatoes are fine in Europe; in the USA they may aid an earworm pest that is common to both. Intercropping maize with sunflowers increases the yields of both. Brussels sprouts do best of all the brassicas with maize. Kale, Savoy cabbages and broccoli can also be interplanted, as when the sweet corn is cleared in early autumn it allows them a final spurt of growth before winter. Maize contains allelopathic compounds that check root growth in annual weeds and suppresses clover and dandelions in lawns. Dressings of the flour also stimulate growth in the grass. Maize uses pollen to prevent nearby plants setting viable seed; just ten grains of their pollen on the stigma of other plants is enough to do this!

Specific companionships well worth employing or avoiding in the fruit cage and orchard

Often, these two areas are occupied almost solely by the fruiting plants, though usually an orchard will have a turf sward. As these are trees and shrubs they are very competitive and are rarely bothered by other sorts of plants underneath, but judicious planting of known companions can significantly improve crops by bringing in pollinators and predators, and some others can increase the vigour and disease resistance of the crops. Most fruits are benefited by alliums, stinging nettles, nasturtiums, tansy, southernwood and horseradish growing nearby. A tea of valerian was used to stimulate flowering in fruit trees when sprayed on in spring. Alfalfa, clover and other legume seeds should be mixed in with the grass seed when orchards are grassed down.

Apples benefit from wallflowers and suffer less scab when alliums, especially chives, are grown underneath the trees. Penstemons planted beneath repel sawfly and nasturtiums discourage woolly aphid. Apples give off ethylene gas as they ripen which affects plants nearby, in particular causing neighbouring potatoes to be prone to blight.

Black walnut (*Juglans nigra*) leaves stop other plants around them growing, particularly potatoes, tomatoes, apples and blackberries.

Blackberries provide a sacrificial crop as grapes ripen, while they benefit from tansy and stinging nettles.

Figs do badly near rue.

Gooseberries benefit from underplanting with *Limnanthes douglasii* or chickweed. Tomatoes aid them and broad beans drive away their sawfly caterpillar.

Grapes are supposedly made sterile by Cypress spurge (*Euphorbia cyparissias*); they dislike laurels, radishes and cabbages and possibly horseradish. Traditionally supported on elms or mulberries, they also benefit from blackberries, hyssop and mustard nearby.

Raspberries benefit moderately when underplanted with tansy, garlic or marigolds. They may encourage blight on potatoes nearby.

Strawberries get improved disease resistance if onions are interplanted, yet the plants grow poorly around them. Strawberries can have an intercrop of any beans, especially French, which do well with them, or spinach and lettuce. They are aided by chrysanthemums, and borage is their best companion. Strawberries grow well at the base of peach trees and raspberries, but not right under them. Plantains nearby are bad as hosts to strawberry aphids. Strawberries love mulches of pine needles, but avoid oat straw as this may cause root rots.

Plums should not be planted near anemones as they share a rust disease.

Rhubarb stalk pieces are reputed to control clubroot and root flies in brassicas if they are included in the planting hole; sadly, so far, tests have shown only little benefit. Mice show much distaste to extract of rhubarb root.

Specific companionships well worth employing or avoiding in the flower garden

Although there is little information on many ornamentals, most will benefit from legumes grown amongst them, but only a few specific companion interactions are recorded. Crotalaria, castor oil plants, pot marigolds, Tagetes marigolds, sages, petunias and dahlias are all useful plants to include in a border as each hinders varieties of eelworm.

Right: The flower garden benefits from French marigolds, too

Aquilegias have less red spider mites if rhubarb is nearby.

Chrysanthemums close to alliums, or even following in the same soil as onions, will grow small and flower prematurely.

Gladioli don't get on with peas and beans, nor possibly with sweet peas either.

Lupins suppress weeds, especially fat hen, and dislike buckwheat.

Roses are protected from blackspot by tomatoes and alliums, especially chives and garlic. Lavender or parsley underneath roses keep down aphids as will garlic. Parsley, mignonette, lupins and *Limnanthes douglasii* are also beneficial to roses, whilst box and privet hedges are not. The boiled leaves of rhubarb have been long used against aphids and against blackspot on roses.

Nasturtium (*Tropaeolum majus*) has a strong smell which camouflages other plants from pests and drives many pests away.

Pelargonium, the tender houseplant not the wild cranesbill, has very pongy foliage, those with lemon or ginger scents especially, and this will hide other plants. The white-flowered form is said to be good for maize. In the USA they have also been used to discourage cabbage worms and beetles and as sprays against cabbage moths, corn earworms and Japanese beetles.

Valerian (*Valeriana officinalis* not centranthus), is generally helpful and beneficial and encourages earthworms but attracts cats. It stimulates composting and accumulates phosphorus.

Pittosporum, like wormwood, is said to be bad for everything else near it.

Left: Valerian is good for encouraging earthworm, and feline, activity

Specific companionships well worth employing or avoiding under cover

Here again there has been little research into specific companion interactions, so those known from tropical situations are included.

Aubergines grow well with peas, tarragon and thymes.

Citrus trees are aided by rubber, oak and guava bushes and are protected from ants by *Aloe vera* but inhibited by convolvulus. Their peel has been used for sprays against fall armyworms and bollworms (an American pest).

Cucumbers like legumes, dill, beet and carrots, mutually dislike potatoes and most strong herbs, especially sage. They may attract whitefly off tomatoes. Stinging nettle tea prevents downy mildew and extracts of garlic and horsetail (equisetum) control powdery mildew.

Melon seed germinates better when sown with Morning glory (ipomea). Melons like sweet corn, peanuts and sunflowers, but not potatoes.

Sweet and hot peppers are prone to aphids, but the extract of hot chilli pepper made from the dried fruit and seeds is effective at discouraging these and many other pests. Some chillies have root exudates that inhibit Fusarium diseases. Peppers like basil, which grows well with them, but dislike radishes and kohlrabi.

Tagetes marigolds should be by every door and window to prevent whitefly coming in.

Tomato root exudates inhibit lettuce, radish and cucumber plants, so never plant these together. Rue prevents tomato seeds from germinating. Tomatoes get on well with basil, alliums, marigolds and nasturtiums and particularly well with asparagus.

Bold: Sweet corn and running French beans combine well together, even under cover

The future of companion planting

What is possible? It is apparent that with tens of thousands of plants to investigate, the number of potential combinations are statistically frightening. However, observant gardeners have noticed the many good and bad interactions discussed so far and we can at least start from here.

There seems no doubt that companion planting effects exist and that we can employ them for our own ends. What we are looking for is more automatic pest control and effective disease control. The first may be more easily achievable; it seems the natural checks and balances on pests can be improved and the desired plants protected by many different plant companions in a host of ways. With a plethora of trap plants, sacrificials, camouflage smells and other plants encouraging more beneficial insects we should easily be able to keep pests within bounds.

Air-borne diseases may be more difficult to control; however, the improved vigour and natural resistance good companions can confer will help. This is increasingly so as we discover more about the organisms living on the plants' surfaces and how their populations are altered by companion plants. Soil-borne diseases may prove easier to control in future as they are so significantly influenced by plant exudations and soil organisms, both of which we could learn to manipulate more fully.

Perhaps the most important discoveries will be about specific combinations that enhance production by eliminating bottle necks at the microscopic scale. The micro-life in the soil and on the plants' surface exist in huge numbers, but relative to their scale they are often rather scarce. It is said that on most soil particles the life is about as concentrated as in desert lands.

Perhaps we can select plant combinations that will bring this microcosm to the intensity of a savannah or woodland instead, then our gardens will flourish in ways we have never dreamed possible.

Above: The Shoofly plant (nicandra) may prove as useful as marigolds - especially if a dwarf form can be bred

Appendices
Appendix I

Summary of companion effects on the vegetable bed

Beans, Broad, Tic and field – Do better with brassicas, carrots, celery, cucurbits, potatoes, summer savory and most herbs. Do less well with alliums.

Beans, French – Do better with celery, cucurbits, potatoes, strawberries and sweet corn. Do less well with alliums.

Beans, Runner – Do better with sweet corn and summer savory. Do less well with beetroot and chards, and kohlrabi.

Beetroot and chards – Do better with most beans, brassicas, alliums, kohlrabi, parsnips, turnips and swedes. Do less well with runner beans.

Brassicas, cabbage family – Do better with beetroot and chards, celery, dill, nasturtiums, alliums, peas and potatoes. Do less well with runner beans and strawberries.

Carrots – Do better with chives, leeks, lettuce, alliums, peas and tomatoes.

Celery and celeriac – Do better with brassicas, beans, leeks and tomatoes.

Cucurbits (cucumber, courgette, marrow, melons, pumpkins and squashes) – Do better with French and runner beans and sweet corn. Do less well with peas, broad beans, nasturtiums and potatoes.

Leeks – Do better with carrots, celery and onions.

Lettuce – Do better with carrots, cucurbits, radish, strawberries and chervil.

Alliums – Do better with beetroot and chards, lettuce, strawberry, summer savory and tomatoes. Do less well with legumes.

Peas – Do better with beans, carrots, cucurbits, sweet corn, turnips and potatoes. Do less well with alliums.

Potatoes – Do better with peas, beans, brassicas, asparagus and sweet corn. Do less well with tomatoes and cucurbits.

Sweet corn – Do better with legumes, brassicas, cucurbits, potatoes and sunflowers.

Sweet and chilli peppers – Do better with basil. Do less well with kohlrabi, and radishes.

Sunflowers – Do better with cucurbits and nasturtiums. Do less well with potatoes, runner beans, sweet corn and grasses.

Tomatoes – Do better with asparagus, basil, carrots, brassicas, alliums and parsley. Do less well with kohlrabi and potatoes.

Turnips and Swedes – Do better with peas.

Left: Potatoes do well with peas

Appendix II:

Weeds known to be much visited by insects, thus likely to enhance predator parasite and pollinator levels

Anthriscus sylvestris – wild chervil flowers have been recorded as visited by 73 species of insect.

Carduus acanthoides – welted thistle visited by 44 different insect species.

Centaurea jacea/nigra – knapweed visited by at least 48 different insect species, of which more than a dozen were Lepidoptera species (butterflies). Out of every 100 visitors to the flowers, 58 are bees, 27 butterflies and moths and 12 flies.

Chaerophyllum temulum – rough chervil flowers have been recorded as visited by 23 species of insect.

Chrysanthemum leucanthemum – ox-eye daisy is visited by 72 different insect species.

Cirsium arvense and others – thistle may be unwanted companions in many ways but they're visited by 88 different insect species, including many butterflies.

Eupatorium cannabinum – hemp agrimony is a weed of damp places and is visited by 18 different insect species, over half of which are Lepidoptera.

Heracleum sphondylium – hogweed flowers have been recorded as visited by an astounding 118 species of insect.

Picris hieracioides – bristly ox tongue is visited by at least 27 different insect species.

Senecio jacobaea – ragwort is dangerous to livestock, causing liver cancer, but it is beneficial to insects and is visited by 49 different species, predominantly bees and flies.

Taraxacum officinale – dandelion is host to predatory wasps and attracts at least 93 different insect species, unfortunately including mangold fly (*Pegomyia betae)*, a serious pest of turnips.

***Vicia* spp.** – vetches attract aphids which are particularly good for improving the fertility of ladybirds.

Above: Ox-eye daisies and dandelions are certainly weeds but also great for encouraging insects

Appendix III:

Herbs that have distinct companion effects (including against some American pests not yet arrived here)

Allium schoenoprasum – chives, en masse, suppress fungal diseases, especially blackspot on roses and scab on apples. They discourage aphids on chrysanthemums, sunflowers and tomatoes and benefit carrots. Chive sprays have been used against downy and powdery mildew on cucumbers and gooseberries.

Anthemum graveolens – dill is not liked by carrots but aids cabbages, lettuce, onions, sweet corn and cucumber, and repels aphids and spider mites.

Armoracia rusticana – horseradish may aid potatoes, but it is bad for grapes and accumulates calcium, potassium and sulphur. In the USA it is used against Blister and Colorado beetles. The tea has been used against brown rot in apples.

Artemesia spp. – this genus contains many plants with insecticidal properties. Wormwood (*A. absinthium*) is strongest and is detested by almost all other plants; its presence seriously reduces yields of brassicas and hinders caraway, fennel and sage, but it does supply nectar for bees and hoverflies and when used as a spray discourages many pests, including cats and dogs. Do not put wormwood on the compost heap as it may slow down the process. Southernwood (*A. abrotanum*) is a milder relative that discourages moths and insects; it is not so universally disliked as wormwood so it is useful in borders as a pest deterrent, particularly for brassicas and carrots. Mugwort (*A. vulgaris*) seed is supposedly liked by hens and may help control their lice and worms.

Borago officinalis – borage is one of the best bee plants and, as a good accumulator of minerals, it makes an excellent liquid feed – better than comfrey, as it is richer in magnesium and nitrogen. Benefits strawberries. Used to reduce attacks of Japanese beetles and tomato hornworms.

Calendula officinalis – pot marigolds are beneficial to many insects and plants and supposedly repel dogs from their vicinity.

Sprays have been used against asparagus beetles and tomato hornworms.

Coriandrum sativum – coriander repels aphids and attracts bees. It has been used as a spray against spider mites. It helps germinate anise but hinders fennel.

Foeniculum vulgare – fennel has inhibitory effects on beans, caraway, kohlrabi and tomatoes, dislikes coriander and, like almost every other plant, detests wormwood. Fennel is host to hoverflies and predatory wasps and may deter aphids.

Hyssopus officinalis – hyssop is a superb bee plant which makes lovely honey; it benefits grapevines and deters cabbage butterflies, but radishes don't like it.

Laurus nobilis – bay inhibits grapes.

Lavendula officinalis – lavender is used to keep pests out of clothes and keeps some away from the garden, especially aphids from roses.

Marrubium vulgare – horehound stimulates and aids fruiting in tomatoes.

Mentha spp. – mints will grow under walnuts, thrive near stinging nettles and help cabbage and tomatoes. Their smell repels rodents, clothes moths, fleas and flea

beetles and spearmint discourages aphids by discouraging their 'owners', the ants. Sprays of mint tea repel ants and Colorado beetle. Mints are good autumn bee plants and also aid hoverflies and predatory wasps.

Mentha x piperita – peppermint oil is much used for scent and flavour. The production is improved by the presence of stinging nettles but, when alongside chamomile, it is reduced while the productivity of chamomile increases. Like other mints, peppermint will help brassicas stay free from cabbage white butterfly

Above: Chives are excellent companions with most plants, other than legumes

caterpillars. Loved by bees and other beneficial insects. Peppermint extracts significantly reduce infestations of clubroot fungus of brassicas.

Mentha pulegium – pennyroyal is beneficial to brassicas and long used as a personal, home and garden insect repellent.

Ocimum basilicum – basil goes well with tomatoes and makes a trio with asparagus. It has been sprayed as an emulsion against asparagus beetle and used as a trap plant for aphids. Basil dislikes rue.

Origanum spp. – marjoram and oregano are beneficial plants that have a strong aromatic oil that gives some control over botrytis and grey mould.

Petroselinum hortense – parsley aids tomatoes and asparagus, making a happy trio (note: some varieties of tomato may not get on with parsley). Used to mask carrots and onions from their root flies, it suffers from carrot root fly itself so it is also acting as a sacrificial. Parsley tea deters asparagus beetles. Loved by bees and hoverflies and when planted under roses parsley repels their aphids. Parsley seeds contain antibiotics to protect them from botrytis; liquid extracts are protective to French beans. Sow parsley to attract hares.

Rosmarinus spp. – rosemary efficiently deters seeds germinating beneath the plants.

Ruta graveolens – rue gets on badly with basil but mutually likes figs, prevents lettuce and tomato seeds germinating and is bad for courgettes and cauliflowers. Its smell drives away fleas, Japanese beetles and many flying pests.

Salvia officinalis – sage inhibits cucumbers, likes rosemary, and dislikes rue. The smell protects Brassicas from many pests.

Satureja hortensis – summer savory (winter savory is similar) protects broad beans from blackfly/aphids and beetles and gets on with onions. Summer savory exudates significantly reduce infestations of clubroot fungus of brassicas.

Tanacetum vulgare – tansy was traditionally used for ants. (Maybe it was originally 'Antsy', as butterflies were flutter-bys.) The dried herb deters clothes moths and other household pests. Tansy accumulates potassium and is beneficial in orchards, getting on with most berries, roses and grapes. Tansy is host to ladybirds and visited by at least 27 different insect species, including five Lepidoptera. Tansy spray is used against aphids, cabbage worms,

Colorado beetles, Japanese beetles, striped cucumber beetles and squash bugs.

Thymus spp. – thyme is a protective plant, and great for bees! Thyme teas have been used to deter cabbage loopers, cabbage worms and whiteflies. Exudates from thyme significantly reduce infestations of clubroot fungus of brassicas and the extracted oil controls botrytis and grey mould.

Valeriana officinalis (not centranthus) – valerian is generally beneficial; it stimulates composting, encourages worms, attracts cats and accumulates phosphorus. Valerian tea stimulates flowering in fruit trees.

Above: Rosemary and thyme are especially valuable herbs in flower

Appendix IV:

Mineral-accumulating weeds (* those edible in moderation)

Achillea millefolium – yarrow accumulates copper, magnesium, nitrogen, phosphorus, potassium.

Anagallis arvensis – scarlet pimpernel accumulates calcium.

Anthemis arvensis – corn chamomile accumulates calcium, potassium.

***Bellis* spp.** – daisies accumulate calcium, magnesium.

Capsella – Shepherd's Purse accumulates calcium.*

Chenopodium album – fat hen accumulates calcium, iron, nitrogen, phosphorus, potassium, sulphur.*

Chrysanthemum segetum – corn marigold, accumulates calcium, phosphorus.

Cichorium intybus – chicory accumulates magnesium, potassium.*

***Cirsium* spp.** – thistles accumulate potassium.

Datura stramonium – thornapple accumulates phosphorus, potassium.

Digitalis purpurea – foxgloves accumulate iron.

Euphorbia helioscopia – sun spurge accumulates boron.

Galium aparine – goosegrass accumulates calcium, potassium.

***Plantago* spp.** – plantains accumulates cobalt, magnesium, potassium, silica.

Portulaca – purslane accumulates calcium, nitrogen, phosphorus, potassium, sulphur.*

Potentilla anserine – silverweed accumulates calcium, iron, magnesium.

Poterium sanguisorba – salad burnet accumulates magnesium.*

Rumex acetosella – sheep's sorrel accumulates phosphorus.

Senecio vulgaris – groundsel accumulates iron, nitrogen.*

***Sonchus* spp.** – sowthistles accumulate

copper, nitrogen*

Stellaria media – chickweed accumulates copper, iron, manganese, nitrogen, potassium. *

Symphytum officinale – comfrey accumulates potassium.

Tanacetum spp. – tansy accumulates potassium.

Taraxacum spp. – dandelion accumulates

calcium, copper, iron, nitrogen.*

Trifolium spp. – clovers accumulate nitrogen.

Urtica spp. – stinging nettles accumulate iron, silica.*

Vicia spp. – vetches accumulate cobalt, copper, nitrogen, phosphorus, potassium.

Above: The rapidly seeding weed sun spurge, a virulent sapped euphorbia, is also a superb mineral accumulator valuably collecting boron

Index